A Pipe Hitter's Guide to the

Citizens Irregular Defense Corps

by Nicholas Orr

A Pipe Hitter's Guide to the

Citizens Irregular Defense Corps

by

Nicholas Orr
Copyright 2021
All Rights Reserved

Chapters

Introduction

As I sit to begin this new book, it has been one year since the release of the *Pipe Hitter's Guide to Crushing the Coming Societal Breakdown.* I am extremely gratified that so many of you purchased and recommended that book. My team and I received a great deal of feedback from you. One of the biggest inquiries that we received was, "When are you going to write the next one?"

To be truthful, when I released the *Pipe Hitter's Guide*, I had no intention of writing a follow on book. Nonetheless, here I am preparing yet another manuscript. During the first book, I collaborated with one of your favorite characters, Thomas Thrasher, as well as a renowned author, Paul G. Markel. For this one, I have already conducted several interviews, both in person and on the telephone with Mr.

Markel and a number of my peers in the pipe hitting community.

As a matter of fact, it was from a telephone call with a veteran Infantry Officer that the idea for this book was born. My initial thought was that I needed to write a thorough article regarding the need to rapidly, but effectively, train members of a community to respond to a local, state, or national emergency. I mentioned to my friend that I considered these late-comers to be a reserve or irregular force. That is when my comrade reminded me of the CIDG *(Civilian Irregular Defense Group)* that was formed during the early stages of the Vietnam conflict.

I was aware of the history of Green Berets training the Montagnard people to combat the Viet Cong. One of my mentors had been a Special Forces soldier in 'Nam who, some twenty years ago, regaled me with tales about working with the indig in the Central Highlands. Also, one of my older relatives was an US Army infantryman who did two combat tours in Vietnam. Among his prized war souvenirs was a fixed blade knife that a Montagnard man had forged from the recovered leaf spring of a truck. That relative had told me of his time working with the native tribes in the II Corps Tactical Zone.

Throughout the modern history of warfare, there have been "Irregulars" trained up by Special Operations Units to combat various threats from communist insurgency to totalitarian regimes to foreign invaders. The US Army Special Forces has as its primary mission the training of friendly personnel behind enemy lines. Though, the Green Berets are not the only organization to undertake such activities.

Military Advisors, regardless of the nation state from which they originate, are tasked with putting boots on the ground and making the most of what they have available in regards to personnel and gear. Unlike traditional or conventional Armed Forces, who are trained at dedicated Military Schools and armed with the latest in gear and weapons, "Irregulars" are trained in the woods, jungles, caves, and deserts. They are armed with whatever weapons happen to be available in that area. In some cases that means nothing more than a sharp machete. In many previous conflicts, advisors have had to overcome not only language barriers, but needed to train locals who had very little formal education or even literacy.

Going back to the early stages of the Vietnam conflict (1962-1963) the CIDG program was a very successful undertaking. Trained by US Army Special Forces, the indigenous people performed well against the communist guerillas and effectively protected their homes and communities from the Red Menace.

One could be tempted to think, "What about the National Guard or FEMA?" Some folks might be willing to default their community's security and safety to external forces. The history lessons we have been taught, over and over, is that any external force that arrives to "help" will immediately, even if they smile when they do it, subjugate the local community. The locals will be viewed by the outsiders as subjects, people to be controlled.

FEMA camps operate as friendly concentration camps where the inhabitants are treated as prisoners "for their own safety". FEMA camps in the United States and refugee camps worldwide are havens for crime, particularly rape[1], and almost immediately fall under the control of gangs[2] or organized criminals.

Even in the best case scenario, external forces enforce martial law on the citizens "for their own good". Citizens will rapidly resent their supposed saviors and dissent will materialize and foment. The greatest hope for a truly secure, functional community is for the members of the community to take responsibility for their own well-being.

My endeavor through this text will be to take the lessons learned from the CIDG in Vietnam as well as Irregular force movements during other conflicts and apply them to our modern world. As you would expect, I will take my three decades of experience teaching Small Arms and Tactics, pick the brains of a number of my peers, and put it all down on paper for your

---

1
https://www.theguardian.com/world/2017/feb/12/dunkirk-child-refugees-risk-sexual-violence
2
https://www.amnesty.org/en/latest/campaigns/2018/10/women-daily-dangers-refugee-camps-greece/

consideration. As an homage to the Green Berets and their students who came before, we will use the term; Citizens Irregular Defense Corps.

Nicholas Orr,

Free America, November 2021

Chapter 1 Citizens Irregular Defense Corps

The Citizens Irregular Defense Corps will be composed of local personnel, often referred to as indigenous or simply "indig" in military parlance. For the sake of brevity, we will use the abbreviation, CIDC, throughout. As discussed during the introduction, the use of Irregulars during states of emergency and protracted conflicts is a time honored tactic and one that cannot be underestimated. Irregulars go all the way back to the American Revolution. Technically, Roger's Rangers[3] were considered to be an Irregular force and their history dates to the French and Indian War, predating the American Revolution.

While it might be assumed that the main component of a CIDC would be young, fit men,

---

[3] https://www.battlefields.org/learn/articles/american-irregulars

of what we would call "military age", that is not always the case. Men, and women, who might not be in the physical condition to serve in a conventional military force, can still be very effective as Irregulars. Men in their 40's, 50's, and even 60's can be effective members of a CIDC, as can mature teenagers who are given proper mentoring and guidance.

The primary qualification for a member of a CIDC is a sincere and genuine desire to protect and secure the community as well as the mental maturity to undergo professional instruction and military guidance. These people must be vested in their community.

For the interest of clarification, let's break the CIDC down into sub-groups;

Security
The CIDC personnel in the Security section will naturally be charged with protecting the

community from all manner of threats. A community cannot function if its members are in constant fear that their food, fuel, etc. are going to be stolen or raided by either opportunistic thieves or organized groups of criminals/thugs or terrorists.

Primary attributes for members of the Security section will be both the physical and mental capacity to be trained in the use of arms and to withstand the common physical tasks that such duties require. Those on the Security team will be required to conduct foot patrols, as well as vehicle patrols. They will be tasked with manning checkpoints and roadblocks. Under some circumstances these men may also be needed to scout or conduct reconnaissance.

It will be up to the leadership to determine which personnel will fit in which roles. As mentioned in the previous paragraphs, community members in their 40's or 50's might not be up to the rigors of patrolling, but they may be perfectly suited to man checkpoints and roadblocks. As a quick aside, the personnel on the aforementioned posts should be mature and even-tempered as the people encountered at a checkpoint will be both good and bad guys. Young men, full of testosterone, have a tendency to be callus and abrasive, that is not the type of person you want interacting with the community elders, wives and children. If you do put a young man on a checkpoint, they should be paired with a mature sentry who has mastered the art of tact.

The Security section is naturally the most serious undertaking as we were dealing with protecting the community from deadly threats. The anticipated threats to the people of the community during a state of emergency are violent crimes; assault, murder, arson, rape, kidnapping, etc. All of these have historical basis and should not be dismissed as *paranoia.[4]* Additionally, the essential supplies of a community; medicine, fresh water, fuel, etc. must be protected from both opportunistic thieves as well as organized thugs and criminals.

Medical

The Medical section must be prepared to deal with a wide range of healthcare situations from common colds and flu to traumatic injuries from

---

[4] https://www.britannica.com/event/Los-Angeles-Riots-of-1992

gunfire or vehicle crashes. Remember, the reason we are establishing a CIDC is because we anticipate a state of emergency where conventional hospitals or urgent care facilities may be overwhelmed or unreachable.

During the civil unrest and looting that followed Hurricane Katrina in the Greater New Orleans area[5], drug gangs and thugs immediately looted every pharmacy they could get to in order to steal narcotics. After the corner pharmacies were looted, the thugs turned to doctor's offices, urgent care facilities and any hospital that did not have the benefit of armed security.

Even after order was secured by scores of armed men, the healthcare system of New Orleans was in critical condition. After looting the pharmacies, the thugs torched them all over the city and surrounding area. The Red

[5] https://www.theblaze.com/contributions/lessons-from-hurricane-katrina-10-years-on-are-you-prepared

Cross and other relief agencies set up tent facilities and had to truck in tons of medical supplies.

During an ongoing state of emergency, healthcare and medical treatment must be localized and protected at a community level if people are to be cared for. All pharmaceuticals and medical supplies must be secured and guarded 24 hours a day.

It will be the task of leadership to recruit and organize doctors, nurses, paramedics, and other first responders into the CIDC Medical section. When a senior doctor or nurse has been recruited, they will be put in charge of the section and given the task of organizing the community's healthcare system. Depending on the size of the community, this may be just a few people or dozens or more.

In Chapter 4 of the first Pipe Hitter's Guide, we go into great detail regarding traumatic first aid as well as dealing with life threatening injuries. Chapter 4 also gives specific recommendations for traumatic medical gear and other essentials.

Logistics

The Logistic (abbreviated as "Log") section of the CIDC will manage community resources. During a state of emergency, resupply will be limited or cut off all together. It is critically important to both conserve and secure fresh water, food, fuel, etc.

If the community is inhabited by mature, prepared inhabitants, most homes will have supplies on hand to care for the families within. However, few citizens have the capability to store large quantities of drinking water and fuel for vehicles, generators, and such. A Logistics section should be led by a mature person in whom the community has an established trust. If it ever becomes apparent or implied that the Logistics Chief is hoarding for themself and their friends, while others are being shortchanged, dissent and internal violence will be the inevitable result.

The head of Logistics must take a rough inventory of communal supplies, without taking control, seizing or stealing in the name of "the common good". For instance, if your community is fortunate to have agriculture, particularly animal husbandry; beef, pork, chickens, etc. the Logistic chief should liaison with farmers and butchers to make arrangements for purchase and preparation of meat. Note: If the farmers and other producers ever feel they are being strong-armed or coerced, they will rebel and the community will suffer. Again, this is why the Log Chief must be mature and trusted by the people of the community.

As you have likely already realized for yourself, for the CIDC to function effectively, all of the groups listed here must work together. The Security Chief will provide armed personnel where needed to be sure that medical supplies, food, and fuel are safe from theft and looting. Medical personnel will tend to the others and the Log Chief will be sure that the community has the water, fuel and resources to support day to day living.

In Chapter 1 on the first Pipe Hitter's Guide we cover food storage as well as the various types of food that should be stored and kept on hand at all times in the event of an emergency or crisis.

Chapter 2 Shotgun Militia

Fortunate communities will have the benefit of citizens who have been trained professionally and are equipped with the gear needed to provide effective security for the neighborhoods. During the American Revolution, the Militias and Training Bands had the benefit of leadership from men who served during the French and Indian War.

Even with a relatively large number of war veterans in the current United States, most communities will be populated by men who do not have the benefit of professional training at arms. During a community, state, or nationwide crisis or emergency, the aforementioned people will not get involved until the threat has materialized locally and is now personal. When people are rioting over food or fuel in the next city over, suddenly, the "average guy" will seek out the veterans to figure out what they can do to protect their town.

For military veterans and civic leaders, you must be able to work with this new source of manpower and understand that they are going to have to "run what they brung" as one of my instructors once opined. During a state of emergency, you cannot give your neighbors a gear list and tell them to come back after they have bought all of the stuff you recommend. No, you must be able to work with what you have.

In the United States of America, and many other modern countries, the most common arm to be found in the home is a shotgun of some sort. Men who consider themselves to be sportsmen and hunters have all manner of shotguns. It is a safe bet that the shotgun is the most prevalent firearm in the USA. Remington Arms has sold over 11 million Model 870 shotguns[6] and O.F. Mossberg is close behind with over 10 million variations of the Model 500 shotgun sold[7]. Folks, that's over 20 million shotguns, not including other brands such as Benelli, Ithaca, Winchester, Browning, and innumerable smaller makers in the hands of American citizens.

Is the shotgun the preferred tool for fighting men in the infantry? No, it is not. However, we are not dealing with a perfect world scenario. In a perfect world, everyone on the security team would be armed with rifles of identical make and caliber. Remember, just like the Green Berets training the natives of the Central Highlands in Vietnam, we have to work with what we have. And, what your community will likely have is dozens or hundreds of average men who own shotguns.

---

[6] https://www.remarms.com/shotguns/pump-action/model-870/

[7] https://www.range365.com/mossberg-500/

The leadership of the CIDC will need a plan to take the common guy with his 12 gauge shotgun and turn him into a person who is capable of fighting off armed gangs of thugs and criminals intent on stealing everything of value from your community. Remember, your enemy already has guns and they will steal even more firearms during a state of emergency.

GEAR: The Shotgun Buffet

Let's consider the easy part first; gear. The professional trainer needs to be infinitely familiar with all manner of scatterguns and fowling pieces. When the crisis hits, your neighbors will show up with a ballistic buffet of shotguns. This will vary from the basic black Mossberg 500 with an 18-inch barrel to the duck or goose gun that will be over 4 feet long. There will be traditional pump (slide) action guns, semi-automatic gas-operated, and double and single barreled models. Hell, someone might even show up with a lever-action blaster. Let's consider these variations from most preferable to least.

Most Preferable to Least

Pump-Action: The pump or slide action is hard to beat as the manual of arms is easy to teach and the guns should consume every type of ammunition from low to high brass. The pump-action design is robust and reliable.

Semi-Automatic: The gas-operated, semi-auto shotgun can be a dream or a nightmare. Top of the line guns, such as the Benelli Super Black Eagle 3, will cycle every load from low powered trap to magnum goose and turkey loads. However, not every auto gun is a Benelli and many gas-guns are finicky eaters and can have a complex manual of arms.

Double and Single Barrel / Breech Loading:
While better than a sharp stick or a machete, even the Hollywood favorite, the double barrel has its limitations. With these guns you get one or two shots and you are out. Reloading under stress is a dicey situation. Yes, I understand that World Class trap and skeet shooters can fire two shots and reload the gun in mere seconds. Nonetheless, the chances that your neighbors are World Class trap shooters are slim. Save the breech loading guns for a last resort.

Gauges

The most preferable gauge is 12. There is no argument that there are more loads for the 12 gauge shotgun in the United States than all others. Even gas stations in rural areas stock 12 gauge ammunition. The same cannot be said for the 20 gauge or the others. The .410

shotgun is a niche caliber and rather poor choice as a man-stopper. Yes, I know all about the specialty loads for the .410, but they are a mere shadow compared to a 1.25 ounce Foster slug or nine 00 buckshot pellets at 1300 feet per second fired from a 12 gauge pump-gun.

There is a reason why law enforcement in the United States has carried 00 buckshot in their duty guns and not birdshot for over 100 years. We have a century of real world, in the field, data that demonstrates that 00 buckshot and slugs are effective man-stoppers. Please save the anecdotal "birdshot for home defense" conversations for your boys at the local gun shop.

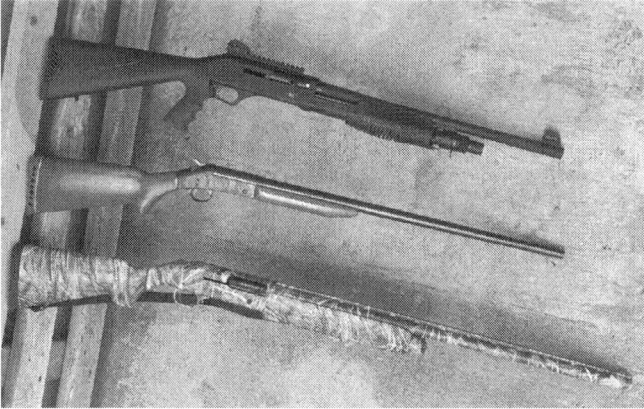

The Shotgun Buffet

Shotgun Owners

Just as you can expect a wide variety of models when it comes to shotguns, the competence and skill level of the shotgun owners in your community will vary as well. Let's consider the various categories and what we can anticipate from a competence level.

The "Owner"

I use the term "owner" in quotes deliberately because this class of folks are the ones who, at some point in their lives, decided that they needed a shotgun for "home defense". These people went out and purchased a 12 gauge shotgun, often based upon price point or the recommendation of the guy behind the gun counter.

Typically, the "owner" bought a box or two of shotgun shells. The gun counter guy likely pitched the home defense upsell and sold the owner one or two 5-round boxes of 00 buckshot. As likely as not, the new shotgun owner took the scatter gun out and fired perhaps a box of low brass through the gun at a piece of cardboard, 2 liter soda bottles or milk jugs. If they fired the 00 buckshot, it is a safe bet that they realized it hurt and only did it once or twice.

The "owner" then proceeded to load their shotgun with 00 buckshot and then staged it in their closet, just in case. It is there that the gun will live for years. Sadly, I have encountered people who did not even go so far as to shoot milk jugs. One man told me, "I'm not stupid, I know how to use a shotgun. Besides, with a shotgun, you can't miss!" That man had purchased and loaded his gun, never having felt the need to fire a single round from it.

The Sportsman

This class of shotgun shooters are those who are genuinely involved in some type of shooting sport. Shotgun sports include; Trap, 5-Stand, Skeet, and Sporting Clays to name the most popular. Yes, for the neophyte, all of the aforementioned are a bit different.

The biggest pro when considering the sportsman is that they have dedicated a great deal of time to mastering their preferred game. They are extremely comfortable with shotguns and understand the intricacies of various chokes, loads, and exactly how their gun patterns. Another logistic advantage of having sportsmen on the team is that they shoot so often that a good many of them have shotshell reloading presses and gear at home. Low brass, trap loads/birdshot are fantastic for drills and practice.

When it comes to weaknesses, I have witnessed many shotgun sports participants who have terrible gun handling habits. They point their guns at their own feet or rest the muzzles on their boots. When the guns are "unloaded" they carry them like a 9 iron or a baseball bat pointing the muzzle in all directions. "It's okay, the gun isn't loaded" is their mantra.

For the sport shooter, their shotguns will have long, unwieldy barrels that are great for sports, but terrible for fighting. Most of their hardware will fall in the double or single barrel category. If they do have a pump or auto gun, most will be set up for sports with limited capacity and perhaps even a "shell catcher" that grabs the spent shotshell and keeps it from falling to the ground. If these are the guns they bring to the table they will need to be modified for fighting, not sports.

The Hunter

The shotgun hunter class is broken down to two subcategories: birds and animals. The bird hunter will be very similar to the sportsman. Their guns are extra long and they have dedicated themselves to hitting a fast moving target. The animal hunter is most often the east coast deer hunter. Due to regulations in several midwest and eastern states, deer cannot be legally hunted with centerfire rifles, instead the "deer gun", a pump action shotgun with rifle sights or even an optic, is the preferred tool.

The benefit of both is that they have real world experience aiming/pointing a shotgun at something living. Successful deer hunters who use shotguns have experience pressing the trigger on a large creature that is going to bleed. That mental experience should not be discounted or shortchanged.

If there is downside to the hunter class, it would be that bird hunters again bring overly long guns, often with limited capacity. The animal hunter as often as not, kills his prey from a blind or treestand, ala ambush. That's not a terrible thing, we will simply need to work with them.

The Tactical Shooter

This is the rarest class of all. The tactical shooter will be the one who has undergone professional training while using a shotgun that is designed for fighting purposes. In years past, many, but certainly not all, police officers fell into this category. Only a small, select number of military veterans will ever achieve tactical proficiency with a shotgun. Sadly, most military shotgun training amounts to a "Fam Fire" (familiarization) and few of those in the military who are issued a shotgun for duty truly master them. Remember, I speak from thirty years experience teaching law enforcement, military, and civilian shooters.

I was present at a military training range when the instructor told the troops, "At close range it is impossible to miss with a shotgun." He reinforced his argument by telling the shooters, "Inside of ten yards, don't waste your time shouldering the gun, just fire from the hip." I have witnesses to back me up on that. I also watched as shooters fired over, under, to the left and right of silhouette targets at ten yards. Yes, you can indeed miss with a shotgun.

If you have a genuine tactical shooter who has dedicated innumerable hours and hundreds, if not thousands, of shot shells to mastery, you have a rare jewel indeed. With some coaching, that man or men can become your assistant instructor(s) or even a primary if they are mature and experienced.

A Proper Fighting Shotgun

Modifications

When presented with the variety of scatter guns and fowling pieces that might show up for your CIDC security team, we need to set some basic standards. First of all, any sport or game conversions such as "shell catchers", "duck plugs" (capacity limiters), super tight chokes, etc. need to be removed. *Note:* There was a time when both Remington and Mossberg shipped their pump action shotguns from the factory with wooden or plastic dowels inside the magazine tubes. Your shotgun owner might not even realize that their gun will hold more than 3 rounds. The good news is these "duck" or "deer" plugs are easy to remove.

When it comes to fighting with a shotgun, extra long barrels are a detriment, not an advantage. More than a century ago, the famous "Coach guns" used by stagecoach guards were merely long, double barreled fowling pieces with the barrels cut down to a more manageable length. Of course, this was long before the BATF and the Gun Control Act of 1934. Today, your shotgun barrel must be at least 18 inches to be legal. If you have a local gunsmith, have him trim down the duck or goose barrels to 18.5 inches so the gun is more practical. Both Remington and Mossberg shotguns allow the user to easily change from a long, hunting barrel to a shorter one. If you have that option, take advantage of it.

Training

Hopefully, you now have a group of men with pump-action, 12 gauge shotguns minus sporting mods, with practical length barrels. If not, screw it, run what ya brung. If you have five guys with single shot 20 gauge H&R guns, again, that is better than machetes.

We will move forward with the training discussion under the assumption that your men have common/similar guns.

In regard to training, as with any mission, leadership must set the standard and ensure that everyone involved understands that which is expected of them. From the very beginning, all trainees should know what the requirements are and what it is they are expected to accomplish.

The first thing that must be drilled into everyone's heads are the 4 Universal Firearms Safety Rules.

Universal Firearms Safety Rules

#1   Keep your Finger Off of the Trigger until your Sights are on the Target and you have made the decision to Fire the gun.
Triggers are not finger rests, they are designed to make the gun go *bang.*

#2   Treat All Guns as if they are Always Loaded
Most every negligent shooting occured because someone *thought* the gun was not loaded. Don't believe me? Ask Alec Baldwin.

#3   Never Allow the Muzzle to Cover anything you are not Willing to Destroy

Before you point a gun and anything/anyone, ask yourself if you would be willing to put a bullet in it/them

#4   Know Your Target, what is around it and what is beyond it.

Bullets/projectiles do not always strike the center or stop in the target, consider what is around the target before you fire.

Notice that the Universal Firearms Safety Rules do not include the words "range'" or "mechanical safety", or "chamber flag". The Universal Rules are, well, universal, that means they apply everywhere; your car, your bedroom, out in public, on the range, and even during a gunfight.

When we are talking about the CIDC security team, those people will be working in and around good guys in the real world. Down range in the world is everywhere. One of the greatest shortcomings of the sportsman is that they never carry a loaded gun off of the shooting line. That mentality leads to the idea that it is okay to fall back on the "it's okay, it's not loaded" thought process.

Your people must be competent and comfortable carrying fully loaded firearms around other people. The 4 Universal Rules are not negotiable. The only time a gun can be considered "unloaded" is after it has been cleared and disassembled for maintenance and cleaning. A disassembled gun is now gun parts.

It must be kept in mind that under stress, people will revert to the level of training they have mastered or what they do most often. If most often, they wave their guns recklessly all over the place, that is what they will do under stress.

Your people must be to keep their muzzles either up or down and keep their booger hooks off of the bang switch. Yes, there is a time for both muzzle up and for muzzle down. There may be things/people on the ground, below waist level that should not have guns pointed at them. There may also be times when there are things/people above your head that should not have muzzles on them. The point is to instill muzzle awareness in your people. They must be constantly aware of what is going on around them and make the correct choice regarding where to point the muzzle of the gun.

This is where you, the leader, must be resolute. There is absolutely no room on a team for someone who cannot follow the Universal Rules. If a person demonstrates during training that they cannot or appear unwilling to follow the gun handling rules, they need to go. If someone makes an excuse for violating muzzle discipline by spouting "it's not loaded" they just told you that they cannot be trusted to handle a gun around other people.[8] We have enough problems during a crisis or emergency not to add friendly-fire or fratricide to the mix.

Do you want to be the one to explain to your neighbor Susan that she is now a widow because Joe, the nice guy who couldn't be bothered with gun rules, negligently killed her husband? No, you do not. Unsafe people need to be shown the door. Give them something else to do, but they cannot be on the security team.

With everyone signed on to the Universal Firearms Safety Rules, we need to get down to the basics of fighting with a shotgun. It is

[8] https://www.nytimes.com/2021/10/21/us/alec-baldwin-shooting-rust-movie.html

during this time that the "owner" category may just outshine the others as they will not likely have years of bad habits.

Thoughts on the Tactical Shotgun

A decade or so previous, I was in a tactical/fighting shotgun class. The instructor offered some words of advice. "The fighting shotgun is one of the most misunderstood tools in the inventory. People either assume they cannot miss or they overthink it. When I look at a 12 gauge pump gun, I think of it like a pit bull, like a guard dog. It is ferocious and mean and it is constantly hungry. If you are not shooting your gun you should be feeding it." I could find no fault in that description and those words have stuck with me to this day.

Basic Shotgun Training Drills

Preferred Target: Genuine steel silhouettes or ½ silhouettes, cardboard or plywood can also be used, though it will degrade rapidly.

Ammunition Requirement: 40 rounds low brass/birdshot, 10 rounds of 00 buckshot, 10 rounds of slugs.

DRILL 1

Preferred Ammunition: Low Brass/Birdshot

Students must learn to control their guns with their dominant hand and work them with their support hand. Left or right handed, this doesn't really matter.

Hold the shotgun securely with the dominant hand on the grip, manual safety engaged, muzzle up, butt of stock against the hip, action open and to the rear, use the support hand to drop a shell into the open action. Close the action with the support hand.

Next, use the support hand to load the magazine tube completely. The number of rounds will vary depending on the gun. When the mag tube is stuffed, place the support hand on the forend. The shotgun is now held in the port arms or high ready position and is ready to fire.

On the command, shooters disengage the manual safety and push the gun out and away from the body, then pull the stock tightly into their shoulder. The upper body is leaning forward, into the gun. Immediately fire one shot on target, pump the action vigorously. Engage the manual safety and return to high ready.

Instructors run this drill until all shooters have expended at least five (5) rounds.

Learning Objectives: Properly loading of the weapon, Operating the manual safety, Mounting the gun, Working the action.

Instructors Note: Many shotgun owners, particularly sport shooters, never engage the safety because they only load it right before they shoot and then they empty their guns before they move off of the shooting point. Others will never chamber a round until they are going to shoot. By failing to fully load your shotgun, you are reducing its capacity as much as 20%.

Shotguns are already a low capacity weapon. Also, and this is a BIG also, people who deliberately keep the chamber empty tend to treat guns as if they are "unloaded" as opposed to "loaded". From this we get the "It's okay, the chamber is empty." thought process and that is dangerous. No one ever had a negligent discharge and said "I thought the gun was loaded." I once had a person ND a gun a few feet from me and then say "I thought the chamber was empty."

DRILL 2
Preferred Ammunition: Low Brass/Birdshot

Hold the shotgun securely with the dominant hand on the grip, manual safety engaged, muzzle up, butt of stock against the hip, action open and to the rear, use the support hand to drop a shell into the open action. Close the action with the support hand.

Next, use the support hand to load one (1) round into the magazine tube. Now place the support hand on the forend. The shotgun is now held in the port arms or high ready position and is ready to fire. Spare ammunition should be ready in a pouch, pocket, or shotshell loops.

On the command, shooters disengage the manual safety and push the gun out and away from the body, then pull the stock tightly into their shoulder. The upper body is leaning forward, into the gun. Immediately fire one (1) shot on target, pump the action vigorously. Engage the manual safety and return to high ready as in Drill 1.

Before the next shot, the shooter will retrieve one (1) round and load it in the magazine tube. Now the shotgun is holding two (2) rounds again.

The instructor will run at least five (5) cycles of this drill.

Learning Objectives: Same as Drills 1, plus reinforcing the need to continuously reload after shooting.

DRILL 3

Preferred Ammunition: Low Brass/Birdshot

Hold the shotgun securely with the dominant hand on the grip, manual safety engaged, muzzle up, butt of stock against the hip, action open and to the rear, use the support hand to drop a shell into the open action. Close the action with the support hand.

Next, use the support hand to load the magazine tube completely. The number of rounds will vary depending on the gun. When the mag tube is stuffed, place the support hand on the forend. The shotgun is now held in the port arms or high ready position and is ready to fire.

On the command, shooters disengage the manual safety and push the gun out and away from the body, then pull the stock tightly into their shoulder. The upper body is leaning forward, into the gun. Immediately fire two (2) shots on target, pump the action vigorously. Engage the manual safety and return to high ready as in Drill 1 and 2.

Before the next cycle, shooters will top off the magazine tube by loading two (2) shotshells to replace those fired.

Instructors run at least five (5) cycles of this drill. At the end of the drill students should have fully loaded guns.

Learning Objectives: Same as Drills 1 and 2 with the addition of practicing a follow up shot and loading multiple rounds to keep the gun charged with ammunition.

DRILL 4
Preferred Ammunition: Low Brass/Birdshot

Shooters will have fully loaded shotguns as they have moved from Drill 3.

Rather than high ready, shooters will hold guns in low ready. Dominant hand on grip, support hand on forend. Muzzle pointed at the ground approximately 12 inches in front of the shooter's feet.

On command, the shooters roll the guns up, placing buttstock in shoulder while leaning into them. The fire command will be given as a number. Instructor says "one", "two", or "three". Shooter fires the corresponding number of shots.

Before the next cycle, shooters will top off the magazine tube by loading the number of shotshells needed to replace those fired. Reloading will be conducted with the shotgun in a high ready position. After loading, shooters return the gun to low ready and wait for command.

Instructor will run at least five (5) cycles, mixing up the commands between 1, 2, and 3.

Learning Objectives: Build upon Drills 1, 2, and 3. Shooters practice running the action and cycling it for numerous shots. Reinforces the need to keep the gun loaded by continuously topping it off.

DRILL 5
Ammunition Needed: 00 Buckshot

*Target: clean/new cardboard or paper target on plywood backing

Prior to beginning Drill 5, instructors will ensure all students understand how to properly/safely download their shotgun. (NO, we do not rack the slide until the gun is empty)

Students are staged 3 yards from targets.

Hold the shotgun securely with the dominant hand on the grip, manual safety engaged, muzzle up, butt of stock against the hip, action open and to the rear, use the support hand to drop a shell into the open action. Close the action with the support hand.

Using the support hand load two (2) rounds of 00 buckshot into the tube, total three (3).

On command, shooters will fire three (3) shots on to the target.

Shooters repeat the loading process of one (1) plus two (2) and go to the low ready position.

Move the entire shooting line back to approximately six (6) yards from targets.

From the low ready, on command, shooters disengage the safety, roll the buttstock up into the shoulder, lean into the gun, and fire three (3) controlled shots on the target.

Shooters repeat the loading process of one (1) plus two (2) and go to the low ready position.

Instructors Note: Have shooters deliberately consider their targets and the pattern spread difference between 3 yards and 6 yards.

With shooters at the low ready, move the entire line back to approximately 10 yards from targets.

From the low ready, on command, shooters disengage the safety, roll the buttstock up into the shoulder, lean into the gun, and fire three (3) controlled shots on the target.

After the third shot, shooters will execute an empty gun reload by dropping the last remaining 00 buckshot shell into an open chamber, closing the action and firing.

*Instructors Note: *Have shooters deliberately consider their targets and the pattern spread difference between 3 ,6 and 10 yards.*

Learning Objectives: Shooters learn to control the additional recoil of 00 buckshot loads. Shooters are given a visual example of the realistic spread of 00 buckshot loads.

DRILL 6
Ammunition Needed: Slugs

*Target: clean/new cardboard or paper target on plywood backing

Firing line moved to 15 yards from targets.

Hold the shotgun securely with the dominant hand on the grip, manual safety engaged, muzzle up, butt of stock against the hip, action open and to the rear, use the support hand to drop a shell into the open action. Close the action with the support hand.

Next, use the support hand to load the magazine tube completely. The number of rounds will vary depending on the gun. When the mag tube is stuffed, place the support hand on the forend. The shotgun is now held in the port arms or high ready position and is ready to fire.

On command, students fire a single shot on target, return to high ready/safety engaged, load magazine and await command.

Instructors run the cycle five (5) times from high ready with slugs.

After five (5) cycles, students move to the low ready position.

On command, shooters disengage the safety, roll the gun up to shoulder and fire a single shot. Students will reload until they have no more slugs in their pouch and then finish the drill with remaining ammunition.

*Instructors Note: *Have shooters deliberately consider their targets and the pattern they have fired with ten (10) single projectile shotgun shells.*

Learning Objectives: Students learn to manage the recoil from slug rounds, understand how to aim a shotgun as opposed to pointing it as they would with birdshot.

Critical Training Considerations

By this time you should see how all of the drills build upon each other. While this is not an overly complex training regime, it serves to fulfill numerous critical learning tasks. Shooters are forced to disengage and re-engage their manual safety on their shotguns somewhere in the neighborhood of 40 to 50 times.

The ability to instinctively disengage the safety and then re-engage it when no more shooting is required is critical to establishing both confidence and competence in the individual shooter. When the time comes to shoot, the shooter must be able to disengage the safety without having to stop and consciously tell himself to do so. If this skill is not mastered, under stress, shooters will be mashing the trigger wondering why the gun is not firing.

As simple as the pump/slide action shotgun is, inexperienced shooters have a tendency to short-stroke the action causing a stoppage or to slowly or gingerly work the action as if they are afraid to break it. Short-stroking is a problem that is likely to materialize in the first few drills and should be worked out by Drills 3 or 4.

Managing the recoil of full powered loads is also critically important. Shooters who have spent all their time shooting trap or light field loads need to understand that they need to place their upper body weight into the gun. We cannot have shooters that are afraid to fire full powered loads. If the shooter takes Drills 1 to 4 seriously and leans into the gun, Drills 5 and 6 should not be shocking.

Drill 5 is important because it immediately destroys the notion that "you cannot miss with a shotgun". Depending on the load and the barrel, 00 buckshot will spread an average of ½ to 1 inch per yard from the muzzle of the gun. Federal Ammunition makes a particularly tight patterning 00 buck load for law enforcement that clusters extremely well. Even off-the-shelf hunting loads in 00 buck will only spread about an inch per yard.

The idea that a single 00 buckshot shell will "fill the hallway" is demonstrated to be a ridiculous myth by Drill 5. Drill 6 is naturally important because it reinforces the need to hold the gun steady with four points of contact: two hands, shoulder and cheek on the stock. With this solid hold/contact, shooters can place single projectile slugs on target, on demand.

Most importantly of all, these basic fighting shotgun drills will give the leadership and instructors the feedback they need to determine which students talk a good game and which ones can actually perform. A person who cannot successfully complete the requirements listed above is not one who can be expected to use a gun to save their own life or the lives of their teammates. Yes, we work with and we coach students and help them correct mistakes. Nonetheless, if a person is still making the same mistakes on Drill 5 or 6 as they were during Drills 1 and 2, they need remedial training or to be given a different job.

Naturally, the aforementioned training drills are meant to weed out those who cannot or will not perform, long before more advanced training is undertaken. Basic shotgun training drills are the foundation upon which we will build a more tactically proficient shooter, they are the beginning, not the end. Training should point out shortcomings, reinforce good habits or performance and provide realistic confidence in one's skills.

During the first book, A Pipe Hitters Guide to Crushing the Coming Societal Breakdown, we discussed Team Tactics: Range Drills in Chapter 3. Although we were generally discussing the use of a repeating rifle in that book, those more advanced drills can be applied to our Shotgun Militia.

The determination to take your security team beyond the basic drills to more advanced ones will be made on a case by case basis. If you are planning to put people on static posts; roadblocks, checkpoints, guard duty, etc. what you accomplished through the basic shotgun training may suffice. However, if personnel will be conducting patrols (also in Chapter 3 of the first book) more challenging and advanced training is a requisite.

Regardless of the specific drills or training that you require your CIDC security team to undergo, the most important achievement is to have men and women who can be trusted to carry firearms around other people and do so in an efficient and safe manner. Again, there is absolutely no room for sloppy or negligent gun handling. Reckless or mindless gun handling cannot be tolerated and must be dealt with directly and immediately. As we mentioned before, we have enough problems during a crisis without having to worry that our own people are going to negligently shoot us.

Training Goals
When you are conducting training, regardless of the specific subject matter, your goal in educating the student can be best understood by considering the four stages of learning and skill development. These are;

Unconscious Incompetence: the student does not even know what it is that they do not know. This is the typical untrained gun owner who says, "I'm a smart person, I'm sure I'll know what to do if I ever need it."

Conscious Incompetence: this is the stage where the student understands that they are lacking the education and the skill, but they have a desire to learn. They realise that they don't know, but they want to make improvements.

Conscious Competence: at this stage, the student can perform the skill as long as they take their time and run through the process step by step in their minds.

Unconscious Competence: this is the ultimate goal for any physical skill. It is at this stage that the student has trained both their mind and body to work as one. It is through Unconscious Competence that the police officer sees danger and without thinking about it, his pistol appears in his hand. When a guitar player can play a song all the way through without thinking about where to put his fingers, that is Unconscious Competence.

Psychologists have explained *Unconscious Incompetence* in a different way, but the idea is the same. In the field of psychology, this is called the "Dunning-Kruger Effect".

The official description for the Dunning-Kruger Effect *is a cognitive bias whereby people with limited knowledge or competence in a given intellectual or social domain greatly overestimate their own knowledge or competence in that domain relative to objective criteria or to the performance of their peers or of people in general.*

Chapter 3 Foreign Weapons

Any Special Operations unit worth their salt will train to be both familiar as well as tactically proficient with weapons other than those issued by their parent unit. Foreign Weapons Familiarization programs can be as basic as an afternoon POI[9] where the Weapons Platoon sets up a few tables and displays captured or acquired weapons all the way up to a week or more of live-fire range training with foreign weapons. I have experienced both.

When many people hear the term "foreign weapons" they assume that means the weapons of the enemy. While that is true, foreign weapons are also those of friendly or allied forces. Most often, Foreign Weapons Familiarization training is conducted with a specific region in mind prior to deployment of personnel to that region, but that does not have

---

[9] Period of Instruction

to be the case. It is always good to have as much knowledge about as many common weapons as possible.

As we consider the CIDC, trainers and leaders need to realize that they are going to encounter a wide array of small arms. We already dealt with one of the most common firearms in the United States; the 12 gauge shotgun. Now we will consider some of the other small arms with which CIDC personnel might be carrying when they show up.

In the previous sections, we stated that the best case scenario is that all personnel will be armed with the same firearms. That situation makes logistics and training so much easier. However, as grandpa used to say, "If *ifs and buts* were fruits and nuts, we'd all have a merry Christmas." We are back to the "run what ya brung" scenario.

Self-loading Rifles

In regards to magazine-fed, self-loading rifles, the well-rounded trainer should be proficient with numerous designs. Of these designs, the Top 5 would be the Stoner-based AR (M-16, M4, AR-10 and variants), the Kalashnikov-based AK-47 (AKM, Type 56, RPK, etc.) Garand-style action to include the M1 rifle, (M1A, M1 carbine, and Mini-14 variants), Heckler & Koch roller-lock actions to include the G3/HK91 (CETME, HK53/93 MP5 and variants), and finally the FN FAL design (STG58, L1A1, C1A1, R1 and SA58). Each of these five rifle designs are different enough to warrant individual study.

Top - Bottom: AR-15, FN FAL, AK47

Top: HK G3, Bottom: M1 Carbine

The "bullpup" category is another kettle of fish. Most of the bullpup styles borrow features from those listed above, though that is not always the case. Common bullpup firearms include the Steyr AUG, Enfield SA80/L85, the French FAMAS, the Israili Tavor, and the FN F2000 and P90 to name a few. In many tactical circles, the bullpup is about as popular as jock-itch, but that does not negate the fact that there are millions in circulation worldwide.

Top: IMI Tavor, Bottom: 12 gauge bullpup

Handguns

When it comes to handguns, once more, if you can master five (5) basic models/action-types you will be well on your way to mastery. The first type is the GLOCK17 striker-fired pistol. Numerous other makes and models are based on the striker-fired action of the G17 to include the S&W M&P, the CZ P10C, Springfield XD(M), Canik TP9 and METE, SIG M17/P320, and many more.

Left: Glock 17, Right: M1911A1

Next up is the traditional M1911A1 single-action. If you can master the M1911A1, you will be well suited to run any of the .45 ACP variants based on that model, the Browning P35 and its variants, the Tokarev TT pistols, and other clones of such.

Top: M9 Beretta, Bottom: SIG P226

Despite being recently replaced officially by the SIG M17, the M9 Beretta can be found worldwide. The uniqueness of the M9 is its DA/SA trigger function and the slide mounted decocker/safety. There are numerous pistols with identical features to include models from Chiappa, Girsan, and Taurus. Also, older S&W

autoloaders have slide mounted decockers and DA triggers.

The SIG P226 and the numerous variants of that pistol again have DA/SA triggers and frame mounted decocking levers. The P226 is a popular military and LE duty pistol and is found worldwide. There are also numerous clones including the CZ99 and the XM9. The frame mounted decocker and trigger design merit dedicated study.

Finally, we must consider the double-action revolver. Though not as popular as they were some thirty years ago, there are literally millions of DA revolvers worldwide from Colt, Smith & Wesson, Ruger, Taurus, and Chiappa to name a few. The cylinder fed, double-action revolver is a unique animal and requires dedication to master.

While the previous list of style and action is not exhaustive, a trainer who has mastered all five of the previous designs is well on their way to overall proficiency with any handgun they might encounter.

Duty and Compact DA Revolvers

Other small arms, such as the numerous styles of pistol caliber carbines and submachine guns are worth considering and closely examining if you have the opportunity. The UZI, the Ingram MAC-10 and 11, the HK MP5, and the Beretta M12 are all fascinating to the small arms trainer. The new Vector pistols, carbines, and subguns from KRISS are very unique and very well designed.

The primary reason, other than being a well-rounded instructor, that a trainer must be familiar with a wide array of small arms is to assess the user's proficiency. One cannot honestly critique the proficiency or lack thereof of a shooter if the gun in question is a foreign object to the trainer.

The CIDC personnel will expect their trainer(s) to be the resident SME(s)[10] when it comes to firearms. If someone does show up with a firearm of which you are completely unfamiliar, be honest and admit that fact. It is better to be honest and say so than to try and bluff your way through the situation. If you try to fake it, more often than not that fact will be obvious

---

[10] Subject Matter Expert

and you will lose the respect of your men. If you don't know, just say you don't know.

Regarding training with and teaching your personnel to safely and effectively use various arms around others, please refer to the Team Tactics and Range Drills section listed in detail in Chapter 3 of the first Pipe Hitters Guide.

Function Check and Test Fire

Regardless of the type of firearm with which your volunteers are armed, leadership must ensure that these guns will actually function when needed. You would be surprised, or maybe you would not be, at the state that many firearms are in. In years past I taught concealed carry training courses. My classes averaged 15 to 20 students per session. I found that I could count on at least one or two guns that the students brought with them not working. Many of the semi-functional weapons had been kept loaded on nightstands or dressers "just in case". When it comes to privately owned firearms, stick with the "I'm from Missouri, Show Me" mantra.

Step one is a mechanical function check. Without needing live ammunition you can test the manual controls; safety, slide lock / bolt catch, magazine release button, decocking levers, etc. You can also test the mechanical reset of the trigger. If the gun fails during a mechanical function check, it goes to the armorer for repairs and we don't need to waste ammunition on it.

After the firearm has passed the mechanical function test, we simply need to find a large dirt berm or a deep ditch that is sufficient to stop bullets and it is not so close to houses that people will complain or be scared. For this test we just want to ensure that the gun functions as expected with live ammunition, we are not sighting it in or checking accuracy. After the firearm in question passed the mechanical and live fire testing, then it and its owner can be off to the range for training.

Before we move on, I should mention that non-functioning or semi-functioning firearms (guns the go bang sometimes) are not just found in the hands of private citizens. During one of my assignments, I needed to qualify with an M-16A3 rifle[11]. I drew a rifle from the armory and when I began my rifle qualification, I discovered that the gun would "double" randomly and without warning with the selector on "Semi". By double, I mean the gun would fire two rounds with one press of the trigger. As you can imagine, when you are trying to make conscious, well aimed shots at a 200yd target, this situation is frustrating.

The problem with the rifle was worn out internal components. My point is, just because the

[11] https://www.armyproperty.com/Equipment-Info/M16A3-A4.htm

firearm in question was on a rack in a military armory does not guarantee it will function correctly. We don't bet our lives and the lives of our team mates on *probably*, we need to know for certain that the tools we will be using to save our lives will work.

Also, every professional firearms instructor should have one or more demonstration or "dummy" guns. By "dummy" gun, we mean a non-firing replica of an actual firearm. When it comes to classroom demonstrations of weapon handling, holster drills, etc. a solid plastic dummy gun is an invaluable tool.

Dummy or Inert Training Guns

Every good instructor has, or should have, replicas or "dummy guns" for demonstrations. There are times during classroom instruction where a dummy gun is a better choice than a live, functional firearm.

Chapter 4 CIDC

Security Assignments

The best way to assess personnel is to have them all undergo the same training regime. It will be during the training process that leaders will be able to gauge the realistic abilities and expectations for the men and women at their disposal.

Training also does more than provide the student with education and physical skills. It is during training that the leadership will observe candidates for the various CIDC Security missions. It is the men's enthusiasm and desire to complete the assigned training tasks, as well as their noted, or lack of, improvement over the length of the training course, that will speak volumes about their potential.

"Out of every one hundred men, ten shouldn't even be there, eighty are just targets, nine are the real fighters, and we are lucky to have them, for they make the battle. Ah, but the one, one is a warrior, and he will bring the others back." – Heraclitus

It has been at least fifteen years since I was first introduced to the above quote. Internet bloggers have disputed whether or not it was actually Heraclitus who said that. The truth is, I don't care if Bozo the Clown said it, the quote is absolutely true, particularly when it comes to military training. For several years, I was a Small Arms and Tactics instructor and often the class sizes were 80 to 100 men. When I applied the Heraclitus "100 men" assessment to the body of men we were sent, it was almost always spot on.

One of the most difficult tasks for trainers and instructors is to not allow the ten who should not even be there to overshadow the nine plus one who will lead them all back home. Trainers often spend so much time babysitting the problem children, that the exceptional ones can be short changed when it comes to mentoring. This is a tough balancing act, but it is essential, nonetheless.

When it comes down to the harsh, life and death reality of the CIDC mission, we cannot afford to be soft or allow our minds to be clouded by emotions. If a person, based upon their performance, is unsafe and unable to meet the standards, they need to be given another job. When we fear to *offend* or *hurt feelings,* we put the entire team in danger and people can and do die, due to the inability or incompetence of the weak links. Every military school I ever attended had a *wash out* factor and that was to be expected. As a matter of fact, I cannot recall a single formal military school that I attended where the number of personnel there on day one was equal to the number of graduates at the end.

The members of the community are expecting the CIDC Security team to be capable and competent. It is not an exaggeration to state that the lives of children, mothers and fathers, grandmothers and grandfathers, are dependent on the ability of the armed security team to stop hostile and deadly threats. This is serious business.

During the evaluation phase, leadership, in addition to disqualifying some who do not have skills, must begin the process of assigning the best personnel for different security missions. Let's take a close look at these assignments.

Static

By "static", we mean that which is typically considered guard duty. Though guard duty might not be sexy, it is critically important to the overall security mission of the CIDC. As mentioned earlier, during a crisis or state of emergency, it is critical to secure the community's resources; fresh water, fuel, food supply warehouses, vehicles, etc. Every community will be different, your community may have a petroleum refinery or a meat processing plant. I should not have to tell you that such are critical assets and must be protected.

Also, medical facilities have pharmaceuticals or narcotics and other supplies that are attractive targets to both individual thieves and gangs of thugs. All medical facilities must be protected.

Some areas that must be guarded will have very few people, such as a water treatment plant, an airfield or a vehicle staging area. Others will be frequented by both the community members and the workers; hospitals, aid stations, grocery stores, etc.

CIDC personnel placed at active, open to the public facilities must be mature individuals who can maintain the balance of guarding the place without alienating those who work there or their customers or patients. Overbearing and authoritarian persons will rapidly alienate the staff and the public. This is, naturally, to be avoided.

We also have static posts such as roadblocks and checkpoints. During a crisis, a community cannot be safe or secure if outsiders are allowed to come and go unchecked. As distasteful as that may sound to some, it is reality. Opportunistic thieves and criminals are counting on you to just let them pass.

Roadblocks and Checkpoints will be frequented by the locals as well as outsiders. The men on these posts must be firm but fair and never make the community members feel as though they are prisoners in their own village or town. This is when older, mature personnel are most useful. While they might not be able to hike ten miles with a weapon and pack, they are the ones who will keep thieves and criminals out of the community. These men are also used as mentors for the younger and less experienced personnel. This is very much like the rookie and FTO[12] system used by police agencies nationwide.

Patrol Teams

Once again, during Chapter 3 of A Pipe Hitters Guide to Crushing the Coming Societal Breakdown, we discussed the 3 basic types of military patrols in detail; Security, Combat, and Reconnaissance. We will not spend much time rehashing that information. Please refer to that section for a refresher if need be.

---

[12] Field Training Officer, an experienced, mature person who trains new personnel on the job.

The CIDC personnel on your Patrol Teams must be in good physical condition and have the requisite strength to carry the basic weapons and gear load without becoming overwhelmed. More than fitness and strength, these men must be mentally sharp and have the ability to make snap decisions in the field. During training exercises you should be looking for men who stand out as team players. Look for the men who are always ready and prepared for the given task. Be on the lookout for those who assist and encourage others, especially students who are in need of encouragement.

There is absolutely no room on a Patrol Team for someone who seems to be in it for themselves or who uses the failures of others to make themselves look better. The "lone wolf" is a worthless team member. Out in the field, every member of the team must be able to rely upon his teammates. The arrogant guy, who is just trying to make himself look better than everyone else, can be put on guard duty or given some other task.

Naturally, those with maturity and experience will be selected as Patrol Team leaders, but every member of the team should have the potential to be a leader someday. The self-starter, the guy who does not have to be constantly told what to do over and over, is the one you want on a Patrol Team. Remember Heraclitus's 100 men? It is the top ten that you are looking for there. A desire to learn and an expressed desire to continuously improve one's skills are both sought after qualities for Patrol Team members.

Whether the patrol is four men, eight men, or a platoon sized element, leadership must have the confidence in those men that they are capable of making sound decisions and executing required actions in the field, minus direct supervision. When we are considering patrolling, we must take into account a wide variety of potential scenarios. A security patrol may go out and encounter nothing day after day, until one day (or night) they run into a gang of armed thugs set on robbing the community.

Conversely, a security patrol may encounter another group of armed good guys from the next community over. Maturity and good decision making skills are paramount in the field. If a patrol hesitates or breaks apart in the face of an armed enemy, CIDC lives can be lost. If they overreact, friendly lives may be lost.

Patrol Team members must be skilled at land navigation, both dead reckoning and directional. They must also be adept at communication and signaling. Most importantly of all, those chosen for a CIDC Patrol Team must be able to gel and come together as a cohesive unit; a genuine team where everyone knows the job of the other man and can rapidly communicate with one another. This does not happen overnight, but with dedicated effort and training, four men who once behaved as individuals can become a very effective team.

React Force

The React Force (or Reactionary Force) is a subset of the Patrol Team composed of members who are not actively involved in patrol missions. The React Force are men who will be staged together in a designated area to *react* to threats and danger anywhere in the community.

A solid, reliable React Force is critical for community security. Your static posts and checkpoints will normally be manned by only a couple or a few men. We don't put a platoon of men on a roadblock as only a few are needed for standard operations and the rest would be stepping on one another. However, if Checkpoint #1 calls in that twenty armed thugs are closing on them, those men need backup and they need it now. Ditto for the lone sentry at the medical aid station who suddenly finds himself surrounded by an angry mob.

The React Force members must know every aspect of the community inside and out. They must know where the critical infrastructure is found and where guard posts, checkpoints, and roadblocks are located. It should also be apparent that in most cases, reliable, dedicated transportation must be staged and at the ready.

In order to keep your Patrol Team members fresh and to avoid burn out, personnel should be regularly rotated from patrol missions to react duty. Through constant community patrols, all members will learn the ins and outs of their area of responsibility. It should also be obvious that team leaders need to conduct *React Drills* or rehearsals. The first time your team sprints to the truck and races to reinforce Post #1 should not be during an attack, it should be done during training rehearsals.

Also important is that the men who are on static posts will have confidence that, should the need arise, backup is only minutes away. This leads to commaradie among all the members of the CIDC Security force.

Camps and Training Areas

As soon as the CIDC is formed and the concept is put into action, designated training areas, camps or buildings will need to be set aside for the function of the CIDC. This is when the training cadre and the community leadership must come together. If the community already has a live-fire training range, so much the better. The person or people in charge of the training range should be brought into the conversation.

If no such facility is available, public or private land will need to be designated for live-fire training. As we mentioned before, private landowners must be compensated. Using some kind of "eminent domain" scheme to seize control of land will only create distrust, anger, and potentially hatred. We already have enough problems without creating more.

Depending on the size of the CIDC Security section, and this will vary from town to town, you might be able to get away with an acre or two with a solid back stop for your live-fire. The training range should be far enough away from residential areas so as not to cause consternation from the people and it should be an area that can be secured from wandering citizens and trespassers. We cannot have the local kids playing on our live-fire range.

The headquarters for the CIDC should be centrally located in the community to allow easy communication and interaction with the civil departments; fire, power, water, police or sheriff. Depending on the size of the organization, the HQ might be just a single office in city hall or it might be a separate building.

A CIDC training camp, on the other hand, should not be centrally located and should be autonomous and away from residential and business areas. Men who need to be trained need to do so without interference or distraction from even well meaning citizens. Again, we may tap public land if it is available or private land after we have come to an agreement with the landowner.

During times of genuine crisis and danger, landowners tend to me more amenable to having dozens of armed men on their property. A farmer or rancher who fears losing their stock to thieves and gangs of thugs may very well greet the CIDC with open arms.

It should be stressed that leaders must ensure that their men always treat private property with the utmost respect. The advice to "leave it better than you found it" is a good rule to follow. Training facilities and staging areas used by the CIDC must be impeccably clean and maintained. Never allow trash or litter to pile up or blow about.

If something; fence, gate, window, etc. is accidentally broken, address the situation and arrange for the repairs as soon as possible. It is far better to approach the landowner and tell them a gate was broken accidentally, but will be fixed ASAP, than it is for them to discover it on their own. Good will goes a long way and bad will festers like an infected wound.

Regarding the React Force staging area, once more this designated place should be centrally located in the community to allow the force to react rapidly to any threat. However, like the camp, it should be autonomous enough to keep the members of the force from being distracted or impeded by the public. It also must be an area that can be secured to keep out spies and thieves.

Also, your React Force Staging Area (RFSA) needs to have the basics, such as; running water, toilets, sleeping quarters, heat for the winter, food preparation area, etc. Your men will be on react duty for extended periods and their basic human needs must be met. Naturally, any camp area you establish must have the same features if men will be living there for days or weeks or even months if required.

Chapter 5 Intelligence and OPSEC

Just as the Security Team must be trained and prepared rapidly, CIDC leadership should begin cultivating and securing reliable intelligence gathering assets from the very beginning. Afterall, the actions taken by the security element, both static and patrol, will be based upon the intelligence and information you are able to collect. Where are the potential weaknesses in the security plan? What is the greatest threat the community faces; lack of clean water, lack of food, theft, gang activity?

Intelligence is about gathering real, tangible, information about anything that could affect your mission. The primary role of the CIDC is the safety and security of team members then by extension their neighbors and community. This mission remains the same, regardless of the problem, crisis, or emergency.

Intelligence Gathering

Intelligence is not just information about enemies or threats. Intelligence can also include information about other good guys and allies. From where are threats coming and whom can you rely upon for aid and assistance?

Intelligence takes into account the condition of the community and area of operation. Have the utilities, including electric, natural gas, and phones been interrupted? What caused the damage and when can you expect the problem to be fixed?

In the aftermath of a crisis or emergency, roads and streets will be flooded or blocked by downed trees and debris. There might be power lines down across a road. You need to know about that. Did flooding weaken or wash out bridges? Bridges don't just rebuild themselves. You definitely need to know which roads are open and which are closed and impassable.

What condition is the community in food wise? Has the public water system been contaminated? If so, where are people getting clean water to drink? Remember, on average there is only 3 days worth of food for the entire community in the local grocery stores. If the delivery trucks cannot get to your town, the stores will run out of food quickly. Let's face reality, panic buying by unprepared people will clean out a grocery store in only a day or two. Rioting and looting will clean it out in hours.

All of the intelligence or information that I just mentioned is valid and important to the Team Leader as it will affect how the mission is carried out. If your local grocery stores have been looted, keeping your neighborhood's food supply safe will be critical.

Sources

The best source of intelligence is direct human intelligence from trusted sources; you and your team. Remember the recon patrol that we previously discussed in the first book, Chapter 3? That is intelligence gathering by trusted sources.

Next comes trusted members of your community. Information gathered from outside sources, such as "the news" on the radio or TV if that method is still working, must be viewed with a critical eye. As we have borne witness to for decades and even more so recently, "the news" is driven by an agenda. Every piece of information from a media source is going to be tainted and skewed to support whatever agenda they have been told to push.

Don't believe me? We just witnessed a television reporter standing in front of cars and buildings that were on fire due to rioting and the reporter stated that they were "mostly peaceful protests". Bottom line, the American news media is not to be trusted to tell the facts, only the story as they have filtered it.

Other intelligence sources can come from real time aerial footage from drones, fixed or rotary wing aircraft if you are fortunate enough to have access to them. In what condition is the airport and who is keeping it secure?

Intelligence can come from neighbors and community members who simply volunteer information. You can and should also cultivate intelligence sources by specifically requesting community members pay attention and watch out for changes or problems or direct threats.

Vetting Sources

Vetting, for those unfamiliar, means a deliberate verification of the information you are given. Unless you have confirmed with your own eyes or your source is historically trustworthy, and sometimes even then, you must endeavor to vet all the intelligence you receive.

Rumor, misunderstanding, exaggeration, and sometimes lies, are all magnified during a disaster or crisis. Sometimes mistakes or misunderstandings are innocent and unintentional. For every additional step taken to deliver information, clarity and reliability is compromised. I imagine that most or all of you have experienced the communication test whether in school or at a work event.

For those unfamiliar with the experiment, several people, four or five, maybe six, stand in a line far enough apart that they cannot hear the other people whisper. A proctor or class leader will read one or two sentences off of a note card and whisper it to the first person. The first one to receive the message whispers it to the next and so on until the last person in the chain receives the message. The last person to receive the message is asked to repeat it out loud. Then the proctor reads the original message aloud from the note card. Very rarely does the original message survive intact to the last person.

How does this apply to intelligence? Let's say a group of four thugs break into a pharmacy downtown. The story might be related between two, three, perhaps four other people before it gets to you. By the time the story gets to you it might relate that a dozen gang members looted the stripmall and beat up store owners. Everyone likes a good story and it is human nature to embellish the story you are telling to make it seem just a bit more exciting.

The story could also go the other way. A gang of thugs numbering over fifty, breaks through the gates and fence surrounding a private residence. The armed homeowners confront the dozens of violent trespassers who, seeing the guns, back down. However, the story that is spun by the news media is that out-of-control vigilantes threatened peaceful protesters with guns. Sound familiar?

The best way to vet intelligence is to get information from numerous sources. Real time intelligence is obviously the best. The older intelligence is, the less reliable it becomes. Also, keep track of, or score, your sources. If someone brings you information that turns out to be overly embellished or just untrue more than once, any future information they bring must be suspect. It is better to get no information than it is to get extremely dated or false information.

Speaking of dated or old intelligence, it should be obvious by now that intelligence gathering is a never ending task. The world constantly changes and situations improve and deteriorate. As a leader, you must do your best to keep up to date with fresh intelligence.

You will also be sharing intelligence with other people with a genuine need to know; Sheriff, Chief of Police, Fire Chief, and community leaders. If you spread unvetted information that turns out to be dated or exaggerated, your reputation will suffer. Never pass on information that you are not as certain as humanly possible is genuine. If you have to pass on partial or fragmented intelligence, tell the other person up front and make it known to them.

Intelligence Evaluation Criteria

The following is a guide to assist you in evaluating sources of information and intelligence that has been brought to you. While not absolute, this is a practical way to consider intel sources as you are deciding whether or not to act upon the information.

Source	Information
Completely Reliable	History of Truth or Verified by Additional Sources
Usually Reliable	Probably True
Fairly Reliable	Possibly True
Not Usually Reliable	Doubtfully True
Unreliable	Improbable
Reliability Unknown	Truth cannot be Judged

Thanks and Appreciation

Hopefully, your father taught you that a good job is its own reward. That is absolutely admirable. It is also true that all humans desire appreciation and thanks. When someone goes out of their way to help you, it is most certainly appropriate to show your thanks and appreciation to them in some manner. When it comes to your team, a good rule for leaders is to praise in public and make corrections in private. If someone does a good job, we acknowledge them in front of their peers.

When it comes to intelligence sources, we do not necessarily want to praise their efforts in public. Nonetheless, you can show your appreciation in other ways. Giving your informants money can seem cheap and dirty. Most of these folks are helping you out of a spirit of community or teamwork. Handing them cash might make them feel like prostitutes. Personal gifts are a better way to go when it comes to showing your thanks. Consumables are good choices for thank you gifts. Coffee, whiskey, tobacco, and chocolate are my go to rewards and "thank you" gifts.

Buying information or intelligence can work, but it is one of the least reliable and most suspect forms of intel gathering. The person providing the information is doing so only to get paid. They will very quickly figure out what they think you want to hear and their information will be tainted in that regard. If you don't believe me, talk to any big city detective who has used undercover "snitches". A desperate snitch will say whatever he or she thinks they need to say to get paid. Sometimes snitches are reliable, just as often they are not. If you are paying snitches, you must go back to the hardcore vetting process, before acting upon the information you get from them. Acting upon intel from a paid snitch without backing it up is a recipe for disaster.

Shared Intelligence
The old saw about the only way to keep a secret is to tell no one, most certainly applies

here. The more people who are privy to confidential information, the sooner it will no longer be confidential. There is a direct correlation between the number of people who know a secret and the time it remains that way.

Why are we keeping intelligence confidential or keeping secrets? Let's go back to the security patrol. Remember how we never run the same route at the same time? Does Karen the neighbor lady have the need to know exactly when and where you will be conducting patrols? No, she does not. All she needs to know is that you are keeping the neighborhood safe. You may need to put up overwatch or counter-snipers in your community. Does Karen, or her husband Kyle, have the need to know where those men are located or even that they exist? No.

People's emotions and morale will be in an extremely fragile state during a prolonged crisis or emergency. Reports and rumors of impending doom and disaster cause people to be frightened and act out of panic. Panicked people do stupid things. Also, it is simply human nature that people like to talk, particularly when they think that they know something that no one else does. Communication is beneficial. Gossip is detrimental. Never engage in gossip.

As a leader, you will receive intelligence on a constant basis. You will need to decide, not just whether that information is reliable, but if it needs to be public. During a crisis, there may be some horrible or terrible things that happen. Will making that information public make people's lives better or worse? It is also your task to destroy or quash rumors and misinformation in as timely a manner as possible. Rumors and false-information can spread like wildfire and destroy the community morale you have worked so hard to foster.

The bottom line regarding intelligence gathering is that it is vital to your mission. Therefore, intelligence gathering is a constant never ending task, and ditto vetting the information you are given. Lastly, you must weigh all of the information you are given and give it value while deciding who has the genuine need to know.

OPSEC

Just as the CIDC will be gathering information and intelligence in order to ensure effective security operations and provide the most safety to the community, the enemy will be doing the same. Yes, for every successful operation there are those who wish to see it fail. In an emergency or a community crisis, the enemy will be opportunistic thieves as well as degenerate criminals who would use the chaos of an emergency to commit all manner of crimes. In the aftermath of Hurricane Sandy, residents not only had to deal with the power outages, but a spike in crime.[13] Although downplayed initially, sexual assault and rape were rampant in New Orleans post-Katrina.[14]

During the crisis, there will be organized criminal activity as well. Criminal gangs may be unseemly and their members troglodytes, but they are led by devious men. These gang leaders will quickly realize that your community has taken steps for security and that you have armed men to protect the residents. While low hanging fruit is available, the thugs will pick that, but such fruit will run low eventually. These criminal leaders will begin to probe and search out your weaknesses. These criminals

---

13
https://www.csmonitor.com/USA/2012/1103/Hurricane-Sandy-s-darker-side-Looting-and-other-crime

14
https://www.npr.org/templates/story/story.php?storyId=5063796

may have family and friends who live within your community.

Another enemy that must be acknowledged is human jealousy and spite. There may be members of your community who feel that, despite being unqualified, they should be in charge. These petty individuals may resent the CIDC or the leadership and seek to undermine it. There will be people who, for myriad reasons, seek to undermine your efforts. One of the most prevalent ways to undermine any operation and embarrass the leadership is to provide false information or fake intelligence. Leadership may be forced to conduct counter-espionage operations in order to weed out the liars.

The vetting process for information is critical for identifying those who may be deliberately providing false information in order to damage the CIDC efforts. We cannot be naive and believe that everyone giving us info is doing so from a sense of community.

Red flags for false intelligence can be unsolicited information that comes from people who have not been asked. No, not everyone who volunteers information out of the blue is lying, but some may be. Also, we need to trust our guts. If information seems just too good to be true, it very likely is such.

Regarding OPSEC,[15] leadership must always be using the "need to know" mindset. If a person, though trustworthy, does not have the need to know details of the security mission, we don't just tell them out of a sense of niceness or friendliness. Every member of the CIDC Security element should be briefed by leadership regarding OPSEC and the need to know. We explain to them that, in the interest of overall security, only personnel who have an

---

[15] Operational Security

absolute need for certain details are given them. This is not "keeping secrets" or "playing favorites" this is a professional, time tested system for preventing bad people from gaining an advantage over the unit.

Other areas of concern for OPSEC are the security of maps with patrol routes, CIDC records, and communication tools. Basic OPSEC includes frequently changing radio channels, altering patrol routes and times, and keeping classified information off of open or unsecure communication lines.

Remember, every email and text message can be forwarded to an endless number of people. Email is NOT a secure form of communication. Logbooks or notebooks kept at CICD HQ must be secured and kept away from prying eyes.

Regarding radio communication, brevity codes and callsigns must be established both to ease and shorten messages and to keep prying ears in the dark. The CIDC G2 or S2[16] will be charged with establishing and then frequently modifying codes and callsigns. During recent history, military contractors conducting operations overseas were given callsigns upon their first day. These callsigns were used as a substitute for their given names throughout the duration of their assignments. It was not uncommon for men who worked together for months or years even, to know a comrade only by their callsign and never even know their last or sometimes even their first name.

Landmarks and features on maps are also given callsigns, number designations, or codes. The large Catholic Church in the center of town might be the callsign "Peter" or "Point 17", anything that is unassuming. Teams are generally given color codes; Red, Blue, Gold, Green, etc. Your React Force might be Blue

---

[16] Intelligence Officer

Team and the Patrol teams are broken down as Gold or Gold 1, Gold 2, Gold 3 if you have multiple teams. You get the picture.

The key to OPSEC is to always assume that the enemy or spies for the enemy are watching and listening. This is not paranoia, this is professional behavior. Interested persons might read the details of Operation Pastorius and the recruitment of eight American citizens of German descent as spies and saboteurs during World War II.[17]

---

[17] https://www.smithsonianmag.com/history/inside-story-how-nazi-plot-sabotage-us-war-effort-was-foiled-180959594/

Chapter 6   Morale

By morale, we will address the mental state of the citizens, both the community members in general and the active CIDC personnel. The morale of the community, whether good or bad, high or low, is a critical factor in the overall success of the basic CIDC mission; that mission being to ensure a secure and well-functioning community. The mission is the same regardless of the population size, be it 50 people, 500, or 5000.

The Oxford dictionary definition of MORALE *is the confidence, enthusiasm, and discipline of a person or group at a particular time.* With that definition in mind, let us consider the morale of the CIDC personnel.

Team Morale
You may have noticed that the Oxford definition of morale did not include the words

happy or *comfortable.* As a person of considerable martial experience, I can tell you that morale can be high or good, even if the men are not happy or comfortable. In the infantry, discomfort is your constant companion and adversity is normally tagging along or not far away. Unit morale can be high, even in the midst of physical discomfort.

Consider the forced march, the ruck march or the hump, all are the same, however the names vary depending on the branch of service. The ruck march or the hump is a physically demanding endeavor that forces the soldier to dig down deep into their mental and physical energy reserves. Men engaged in a hump are not generally considered to be *happy,* nonetheless, disciplined troops who understand that such activity is a part of being a soldier can still have a high morale.

Many novice persons might confuse morale with happiness or comfort. People who have nothing to do, no tasks to accomplish and nothing but time on their hands may be happy and comfortable in the very beginning, but soon their idle hands and minds become the Devil's plaything. For this reason, it is better to focus on the true factors of morale; confidence, enthusiasm, and discipline. During the pages to follow we will consider how all three traits build upon each other.

Confidence in our modern world has lost much of its meaning. People with genuine confidence in themselves and their abilities are often accused of being "arrogant" or "elitist". Of course, the accusers are the C and D students who are either too mentally or physically lazy to put forth the effort needed to become truly proficient.

The other side of the coin is the deluded or an undeserved sense of confidence. (See Dunning-Kruger Effect Chapter 2) These are people who have the belief that their skills and abilities are more or better than hard reality would dictate. Many factors contribute to the delusion. Our "self-esteem" generation is one large factor. Rather than challenge children, students, etc. with tasks that require hard work and dedication, we lower the standards or eliminate the standard altogether in order to make the person in question "feel good" about himself. This leads directly to people who *think* or *feel* like they are skilled, but they are actually subpar.

Recent history has shown this embracing of mediocrity in the interest of self-esteem is not just a problem of the public school system. No, this virus has infected the institutional military as well. Years ago when I was working as a Small Arms and Tactics Instructor I was part of a team attached to a US Navy Surface / Land Warfare unit.

The brass in Virginia were concerned that the rifle qualification scores of the men were not what they should have been. There were too many "Marksmen" (lowest qualification award) and not enough "Experts" (highest qualification award). A Navy *genius* came up with a solution. At the time, the targets being used were a round bullseye-style that had four scoring rings with values of 5, 4, 3, and 2.

Anything outside the 2 ring was considered a zero (0) or a miss. The solution proposed and adopted was to create a new target where the existing 2 and 3 rings were combined thus creating a larger 3 ring. This new target was adopted and miraculously, the scores of the shooters began to go up. I wish I was joking.

Not to be outdone in the quest of mediocrity, the US Army found that a large number of their modern recruits did not have the physical strength and coordination to pass the time honored Grenade Qualification in basic training. Also, the Land Navigation portion, an essential skill for any soldier, proved too difficult for the modern crop of recruits. What was the Army's solution? Rather than expect more of the men or spend time training them, the US Army lowered the standard and eliminated the *difficult* requirements. [18]

Coming back to our discussion of confidence, both examples listed above demonstrate how modern servicemen are being given a false sense of confidence by either having the standard lowered to make it easier or just eliminating the standard altogether.

---

[18] https://starspangledflags.com/us-army-drop-grenade-throwing-requirement/

Real, genuine, earned confidence comes from being presented with a challenge, possibly failing the first try, but meeting eventually that challenge. When I went through Basic Training, we were required to run through the Obstacle Course or "O Course". The most challenging aspect of the course came at the very end; the dreaded rope climb. By the time I reached the rope climb my first time through the O Course, I was exhausted and I failed to get more than halfway up. I failed. However, by the end of Basic Training, I reached the top of the rope with ease. That fact instilled a genuine, real confidence in me.

We must give people greater challenges so they can succeed and build upon those. In order to help men achieve genuine confidence, we move them from the simple task, onto the more complex or challenging and then further we give them advanced or difficult challenges. It is this type of hard-earned confidence that stays with a man and cannot be taken away from him.

Discipline comes from a similar path. From the very beginning, we ensure that our students understand what is expected of them. We give clear instructions and we supervise them. If they fall short or fail, we provide further coaching or instruction. What we do not do is accept excuses from our students. When I failed the rope climb, my Drill Instructors did not care that I was tired. They didn't want to hear my excuses about why I failed. Instead they trained me until I was able to achieve success.

We do not accept quitting as an answer. It is acceptable to fail, it is not acceptable to quit or to make up excuses for failure. Discipline, like confidence, is built one step at a time. A man with genuine discipline that has been earned through effort and sweat and pain is one upon whom we can rely in the future.

Enthusiasm comes from a variety of areas. Often, enthusiasm comes from an early desire to do a job or be something. There are children who decided early on in their lives that they wanted to be a fireman or a veterinarian or an airplane pilot. While many childhood desires fade, there are quite a few people walking around who will tell you that by the time they were 12 or 13 they knew what they wanted to be when they grew up and they did that very thing. From my youth, I always knew that I would serve in the military, even with the distractions of my teen years, I never doubted that I would wear the uniform. When I walked into the recruiter's office, he did not have to sell to me, I was already sold. That is enthusiasm.

Naturally, we cannot rely upon the enthusiasm of our 13-year-old self to carry us through.

"Esprit de corps" means the "spirit of the body" and it translates to pride, loyalty, and confidence in a unit or organization. Esprit de corps occurs when men put the needs of the unit and their compatriots above their own personal or selfish needs. These men are proud to be a part of an organization and proud for people to know.

Again, many moons ago, an instructor advised me that "adversity breeds camaraderie". What that translates to is that men who suffer the same discomfort and hardship will form a bond with each other. A bunch of guys who are friends and spend sunny afternoons on the shooting range will never achieve the camaraderie of men who go through basic training or boot camp together. Men who suffer through pouring rain, freezing cold, blazing heat together, as a team, to accomplish a common mission or goal will form a very real esprit de corps with one another and for the unit.

A part of enthusiasm and esprit de corps is unit cohesiveness. Men who have earned the right to wear a certain uniform or a beret or a unit badge take great and righteous offense at the posers who put on those items without earning them. After proving themselves by undergoing and completing training, the CIDC personnel should be wearing the same uniform, or headgear or insignia. The reality of logistics may not allow for all men to have matching uniforms, nonetheless, some form of insignia should be given to men of the unit who earned the right to wear it.

Curtis Sliwa, the man who founded New York's Guardian Angels, understood the importance of esprit de corps and made the red beret a symbol of the organization back in 1979.[19] This

---

[19] http://guardianangels.org

tradition of uniforms, unit insignias, etc. goes back to the Greeks and Romans and is nothing new. If you doubt the importance of unit insignias to the men who have worked for them; try putting on a Hell's Angels Motorcycle Club jacket that you have not earned, then mingle with a local chapter.

Enthusiasm as a part of morale in a unit also comes from superior leadership. Leaders must have a method to reward those in the unit who go above and beyond. When a man puts forth exceptional effort he should be praised in front of his peers. Remember the leadership trait of "praise in public, correct in private". What rewards or demonstrations of praise you decide upon will be based upon your particular circumstances. There is a definite reason why military units hold public promotion and award ceremonies. Men who are legitimately praised or given an award in front of their peers will have a definite esprit de corps and enthusiasm for the unit.

High morale in a unit also comes from leadership knowing when to drive the men and when to give them a much needed or well-deserved break. This is a fine balancing act to be sure. Men who are driven hard and never given a break will eventually feel that the leaders don't care about them. Conversely, too much down time can lead to laziness or a lack of mission focus. The men should never doubt that genuine hard work and effort is appreciated and will be rewarded.

Long ago, the United States Navy adopted a policy of rewarding men who were at sea continuously for 45 days or longer with 2 beers per man. To the average citizen, 2 beers might seem miniscule, however, to men serving on a warship at sea, 2 beers proved to be a fantastic morale boost. The men felt that they earned the beers and they were an appreciated reward.[20] One close friend said to me, "When you see them loading pallets of beer onto the ship, you know it's going to be a long deployment." My comrade was at sea continuously for 110 days during that particular deployment and they actually had two "Beer Days".

Community Morale

When it comes to taking care of the morale of the community, it is best to start with the basics. There is no point in planning a holiday parade if the people in the village are boiling water to drink and eating housepets. Community morale begins by addressing the foundational needs that every person requires; food, water, shelter from the weather, clothing, and medical attention when needed. Afterall, the purpose of the CIDC security team is to

---

[20] https://news.usni.org/2014/07/01/hundred-years-dry-u-s-navys-end-alcohol-sea

ensure that the community resources are protected from thievery and looting.

Hopefully, the majority of the families in your community will consist of well-prepared households, those who stocked up and stored for the *long, hard winter.* However, we must assume that there are some households; single parents, retired on a fixed income, or those who were just living paycheck to paycheck before the crisis or emergency struck. Community leadership needs to quickly identify these households and ensure that children and the elderly are not going hungry. Volunteers should be organized to check on people in the neighborhoods.

In the event of power outages or the failure of utilities, families may need to gather in community centers or churches or anywhere that can be kept warm and supplied with clean drinking water. This is one of those bridges you cross when you get to it.

After assuring that the community is doing well in the food, water, shelter department, we need to be sure that we have medical treatment available for both emergencies and common ailments. If your community does not have a hospital or 24 Hour Clinic, you might have to turn the fire station into a First Aid Center or the local elementary school or some place that is centrally located. Regardless of the solution you come up with, all of the community members need to know where the medical facility is located. And, going back a couple chapters, in addition to medical personnel, the facility needs to be protected.

Now that we have the essential needs covered, we can focus on keeping up morale with community events. One of the simplest and most effective ways to get people together and build morale is to have a community dinner or barbeque if that is your thing. Once more, leadership needs to organize volunteers to set up such an event. If the weather is pleasant, do it outside in the center of town, if not, use the community center, church hall, etc. Everyone loves the smell of a grill or barbeque pit. The scent of food cooking on the town green will drift through the neighborhoods and lift people's spirits. If you are fortunate enough to have musicians, set up a free concert for the community.

These don't have to be all the time events, but you should try and have some kind of community morale building event on a regular basis if possible. The mental and physical stress of dealing with a community crisis or prolonged emergency will weigh heavy on the public. We need to give them some relief, a chance to forget about the hardships, even for a little while.

Going back to the confidence, discipline, and enthusiasm part of morale, we can instill these in our community as well. Confidence and discipline for the community members come from participating in their own well-being as well as having tasks or duties that must be completed. Everyone should have something to contribute, even children and folks with limited mobility. This is where strong leaders will shine. Good citizens like to feel useful, not useless. The more useful someone feels, the higher their morale will be.

The community members will also have confidence when they see the CIDC security team performing in a professional and well organized fashion. A person who lives in constant fear of criminals and thieves will not have good morale. The community must never doubt that those who are tasked with protecting them are performing to the very best of their abilities. This does not necessarily have to be Tier 1 Special Forces level, sometimes a smile and a "good morning" from the guard at the medical center or the men patrolling the neighborhood is what it takes to make people feel safe.

Nothing can kill morale in a community faster than rumors and false information. Leadership needs to keep a tab on what rumors are floating around and when possible squash those rumors with facts. Those who spread rumors should be encouraged not to do so. Also, it is a good idea for leadership to ask everyone in a public setting to do their absolute best to stop damaging rumors from spreading.

Leadership can help with morale by being honest with the community. If there is a legitimate concern that affects all of the people, it needs to be aired and dealt with. Never deliberately lie to people, even if you think it is for their own good. Eventually the lie will come to light and you will have lost their respect and trust. Also, like any good leader, we don't come to the people with problems or concerns until we have thought of a solution or a positive way to address it. No one likes the guy who brings up problems but never has a solution.

Fitness and wellness go hand and hand when it comes to keeping up morale. The natural tendency of people during a prolonged hardship is to get depressed and sink into themselves. Regardless of the weather, it is important to encourage community members to get outside everyday and take in the fresh air and sunshine. Volunteers can organize walking groups or fitness programs at the recreation center or local church.

Depression and anxiety are very real issues and when people shut themselves off, the problem gets worse, not better. Neighbors should be encouraged to check in on one another frequently. No one in the community should ever feel as though they have to deal with the hardship alone.

Going back to the Civilian Irregular Defense Group during the Vietnam conflict, one of several reasons why the program was a success was that the leadership addressed the grievances of the community. Naturally, such grievances will vary tremendously based upon the community's population and its particular circumstances. Nonetheless, for your CIDC to be an effective and successful undertaking, you must take the time to listen to the members of the community and do your best to address legitimate concerns or grievances.

Chapter 7   Organization and Command Structure

In order for any unit to be successful and effective, there must be a definite command structure and organization of tasks and assignments. The thought process that "we don't need leaders, because everyone knows what to do" is a perfect recipe for failure. The citizen Militias and Training Bands of New England were all volunteer organizations with the ranks filled by community members, nonetheless these units still had elected leaders.

It is true that not every person is cut out to be a leader, some folks serve best as dedicated followers. However, good followers only perform when they have good leaders. Fortunately, we have hundreds of years of military structure and guidance on which to rely. How detailed your organization and command structure will be is dependent upon the size of your CIDC security element.

Beginning with the smallest unit in the military; the **Fire Team** consists of four men.

- Team Leader
- Automatic Rifleman (Asst TL)
- Asst. Automatic Rifleman
- Rifleman

Each man in the Fire Team learns the job of the man directly above him so as to fill in during emergencies or when one man leaves the team for non-emergency reasons.

The next unit up in unit size is the **Squad.** In a typical infantry squad you will have three (3) complete Fire Teams plus a Squad Leader, for a total strength of thirteen (13) men. In the event the Squad Leader is injured or incapacitated, Team 1 Leader steps up to his job, and everyone in Team 1 moves up a tier to take the place of the other man.

- Squad Leader
  - Fire Team 1 TL
  - Fire Team 1 AR
  - Fire Team 1 AAR
  - Fire Team 1 R
    - Fire Team 2 TL
    - Fire Team 2 AR
    - Fire Team 2 AAR
    - Fire Team 2 R
      - Fire 3 TL
      - Fire Team 3 AR
      - Fire Team 3 AAR
      - Fire Team 3 R

Moving up to the next unit, we have the **Platoon.** The Platoon consists of three (3) full squads of men. In the traditional military Table of Organization and Equipment (TOE), the Platoon is the first unit to have an Officer at the lead. There will also be a Senior Non-Commissioned Officer (SNCO) who holds the title of Platoon Sergeant. The Plt. Sgt. is the second in command to the Platoon Leader. This brings the TOE strength of the Platoon to forty-one (41) men.

- Platoon Leader
- Platoon Sergeant
  - Squad 1
    - 3 Fire Teams
  - Squad 2
    - 3 Fire Teams
  - Squad 3
    - 3 Fire Teams

As with the hierarchy of the Fire Team and the Squad, the Plt. Sgt. steps in for the Plt. Ldr. If both of those men are incapacitated, the Leader of Squad 1 takes command of the Platoon and so on.

If you should be so fortunate as to have enough trained and equipped men, we will consider the next unit up, the **Company.** A company consists of three (3) Rifle Platoons which in full strength would be forty-one (41) men each. The Company will also have one (1) Weapons Platoon (referred hence as Wpns Plt). The Wpns Plt consists of crew-served machine guns, mortars, and anti-tank weapons. A full strength Wpns Plt will average 35 to 40 men depending on the unit in question and the crew-served weapons.

The company will have an officer who is the Company Commander and another officer who is the Executive Officer (XO). The XO is second in command of the company. Each company will have at least one SNCO. In the Marine Corps Infantry, each line company has a Company First Sergeant and Company Gunnery Sergeant.

With the four men in Company Leadership positions and the three (3) platoons of forty-one (41) men, plus a 35 man Wpns Plt, that brings the full strength of the Company unit to 162 personnel.

We have not added Medics or Corpsman to the number yet. A well-staffed Company will have one dedicated Medic or Corpsman per squad plus a Medical Team Leader. Think, one medic for each of the 12 squads plus a senior medic who is in charge of the others.

Naturally, all of the numbers listed above for Fire Team, Squad, Platoon, and Company are based upon a perfect world scenario where people are not sick or injured or out of commission for one reason or another. Based upon my three decades of experience, units are almost never at a full strength TOE. It is for this reason that every man must be trained to do the job of the man directly above him. It is that type of mentality and training that has made the United States Military, and others who follow that rule, historically successful on the battlefield. Not every military in the world subscribes to such thinking.

Regarding Special Operations Units that are tasked with training the local population or indiginous personnel, the United States Army fields their Special Forces Operational Detachments to perform such tasks. Let's take a moment to consider the organization of the US Army Special Forces, Operational Detachment Alpha during the Vietnam conflict. Some might refer to this group of men as an "A Team".

- Commanding Officer   Captain
- Executive Officer   Lieutenant
- Operations Sergeant   E-8 (1st Sgt
  or Mstr Sgt)

- Intelligence Sergeant   E-7 (Sgt First
  Class / SFC)
- Light Wpns Leader   E-7
- Heavy Wpns Leader   E-7
- Medical Specialist   E-7
- Asst Med. Specialist   E-6   (Staff
  Sgt)
- Radio Operator Supv.   E-7
- Radio Operator   E-5
- Demolitions Sgt.   E-6
- Demolitions Specialist   E-5

As you can see from the TOE for the A Team, every enlisted man is either an NCO or Senior NCO. The reason for this is that these men must not only be able to perform their given tasks, they must be seasoned and experienced enough to be able to teach others to do so. These Special Forces A Teams, along with SF Operational Detachments Bravo and Charlie (Bravo and Charlie had more men) were able to successfully recruit and train hundreds and then thousands of Montagnard villagers to effectively fight the VietCong during the Vietnam conflict.

The purpose of this chapter is to better assist you in organizing and task assigning men in your CIDC security element. As mentioned prior, the primary security tasks of the CIDC will be static guard posts, patrolling, and the react force.

Depending on your available manpower and your area of responsibility, you may have static post personnel in one Fire Team, patrol personnel in another Fire Team and the react force as a third Fire Team. This configuration would work for a cul de sac neighborhood or small community. For larger areas, where several facilities need to be protected and many miles need to be patrolled, your security element for each assignment would be Squad or Platoon sized.

Men must be organized into team units and taught to do the jobs of the others. Remember, humans are not machines. Your guards are going to need rest, food, and sleep. Sometimes they will get sick or be injured. If a facility, say a hospital or clinic, is important enough to warrant armed protection, we do not leave it unprotected because someone got sick. A man or men will need to be moved in to fill the gap.

Also, the situation during the crisis or emergency may change. If the emergency is prolonged, and resources become more scarce and valuable, the instances of thievery, looting, or criminal raids may increase. While your community was once safe with just a few armed guards and a checkpoint, your security patrols may need to become constant, running day and night. You will not likely have the luxury of time to take untrained people and bring them up to speed when the threats increase. Men must be trained and organized into cohesive units BEFORE the deadly threats materialize, not after.

The sad reality of security is that most people will ignore security or security related concerns until AFTER an incident has occurred. It is all too common for people to adopt the "nothing bad has ever happened here" mentality and then when something bad does happen, they go into panic mode. I have witnessed this situation time and again for over thirty years.

Success or abject failure will come down to the ability of the leadership to properly evaluate the strengths of the men, to train them thoroughly, and to organize them effectively. The goal of the leadership of any unit is to have men who are prepared to do what is needed without having to be told exactly what to do and when to do it.

General George Patton was one of the most successful, potentially *the* most successful, combat leaders that the United States ever had. One of Patton's leadership philosophies was to ensure that the men were rigorously trained, were given the overall mission statement and tactical goals, and then he put them in a position where they could exercise sound judgment and take charge to accomplish this mission.

For instance, if a city or a town needed to be taken, Patton would give his leadership the mission of taking the town, but he would not tell them how to take it. Patton had faith in his battlefield commanders and he expected them to exercise sound judgment and initiative to achieve the goal. Patton's leadership philosophy was proven to be sound and correct, time and time again during World War II. [21]

---

[21] https://amzn.to/31xqB14

CIDC Medical Section

Just as the Security section must have a definitive structure and organization, so must the Medical section. How this structure is composed will be largely dependent upon the size of the community and the available personnel. As we discussed in the previous paragraphs of this chapter, you may only have a few trained and experienced personnel. Regardless, someone needs to be in charge and be given the task of organizing the others.

Positions of leadership in the Medical section will naturally be given to those with the highest level of education and years of experience. It would not make sense to put a volunteer EMT in charge when a trauma surgeon with twenty years experience is available. Let's examine some possible scenarios for Medical team structure.

Small Team

- Team Leader (Doctor, Paramedic, ER Nurse)
- Asst. Team Leader (person will ability to step in as leader)
- Field Medic / Corpsman
- Asst. Field Medic

Community Team

- Medical Team Chief (Doctor, Paramedic, ER Nurse)
- Asst. Medical Chief (person will ability to step in as leader)
  - Aid Station Leader
  - Asst. Aid Station Leader
  - Nurses
  - Specialists
  - Medics
  - Volunteers
    - Field Medic Leader

- Asst. Field Medic Leader
- Field Medics

The preferred situation would be for the Medical section to have enough personnel to operate a clinic, aid station, or even a hospital while also having enough trained people to create a Field Medic section. The Field Medics will work directly with the CIDC security teams and at least one medic will accompany the men on patrols. Field Medics will also act as an ambulance / paramedic force to respond immediately to emergency medical situations that may arise anywhere in the community. Most small communities in the United States have dedicated, whether paid or volunteer, squads or ambulances already and that is a tremendous asset to the citizens.

What will be the most unusual or strange situation for conventional medical personnel is to be put in the role of a field medic or a corpsman accompanying armed security personnel. During routine living, the men on squads or ambulances are ordered as a matter of course to never go into a situation where forces are actively engaged in fighting. It is for this reason that SWAT teams have adopted and trained SWAT Medics to accompany teams.

If your small community has trained a SWAT medic or military veteran medic or corpsmen, consider yourselves fortunate. If not, you will need to choose from those who are physically fit and able to travel great distances on foot and think on their feet.

Chapter 8 Specialists

In addition to personnel upon whom you can rely to man guard posts, secure facilities, run check-points or roadblocks and conduct patrolling activities, you may require specialists. In this chapter we will consider some of the specialists whom the leadership might seek out and employ.

Tradesmen

During a prolonged crisis or emergency, your community will require the skills of tradesmen. By tradesmen we mean large and small engine mechanics, welders, carpenters, electricians, plumbers and engineers. Vehicles will need to be repaired and maintained. Both public and private facilities will certainly need maintenance and repair due to either natural wear and tear or criminal damage or sabotage.

Keep in mind, the entire purpose of this text is to prepare communities to be self-sufficient and to function without the need for external assistance, because external assistance cannot be relied upon. Tradesmen, such as those mentioned, will be critical during a community, state, or nationwide emergency.

Although not a professional trade, HAM radio operators and those experienced with radio communication should be sought out. Unlike the internet and mobile phones, HAM radio is not dependent upon an external network or service program. Even if the internet or the local phone grid crashes, HAM radio will still function. An added benefit of many dedicated HAM operators is that they generally have a plethora of comm gear and the experience to maintain and repair it.

Military Veterans

Whether recently discharged or seasoned, veterans will be an invaluable asset to the CIDC program. The value of Infantry veterans with combat experience is a given for the security element of the CIDC. However, we must not overlook other veteran specialists such as those trained in; Communications, Engineering, Logistics and Supply, Heavy Equipment Operators, Aircraft Mechanics and many others. It is incumbent upon leadership to seek out and identify military veterans and vet them in regard to their various skills.

Does your community have a municipal airport? Both fixed and rotary wing aircraft are tremendous assets during a crisis, whether they are commercial or privately owned. Aircraft require continued maintenance and care. They need people to fuel them and airports need someone to be in control. During a crisis, you cannot rely upon specialists who might live hours away.

Amongst your veterans, you may have various warfare specialists; Cold Weather, Mountain, Desert, MOUT[22], Water Operations, (can your community be accessed via a lake or river?) etc. We don't just fight when the weather is nice or pleasant. Bad guys will not be *fair* or *courteous* and only attack you on sunny afternoons. The CIDC must be prepared to function in all weather conditions, in the daytime and under cover of darkness. All of the aforementioned specialties require study and training to master. The most valuable asset that the aforementioned military veterans will have is experience operating in such environments. You cannot buy experience and its value should not be understated.

---

[22] https://www.hsdl.org/?view&did=457801

Hunters and Field Scouts

During the previous Pipe Hitter's Guide, we discussed the value of the reconnaissance or the recon patrol. If you are so fortunate to have military veterans skilled at recon or scouting, consider yourself lucky. If not, you may enlist the assistance of hunters with a lifetime of experience moving quietly and stealthily in the field. We are discussing the kind of hunter who understands how to read the wind, game sign, can navigate with a map and compass as well as dead reckoning, understands the weather and how to operate in poor conditions. This is the kind of man who can get within fifty yards of a mature buck and take it down.

Recon patrols can be a critical tool for leadership to gain real world intelligence. The men tasked with such duty must be able to move stealthily and unseen. Remember, the primary purpose of a recon patrol is to gather information, not engage in combat. Recon patrol members must be able to make good decisions in the field without external guidance. They also must be mature enough to know when to fight and when to make a tactical withdrawal. Your hunters may also be tasked as trackers should the situation warrant.

Counter-Snipers / Overwatch

The history of civil unrest both in the United States and overseas has shown that hostile forces will definitely make use of snipers. In November of 2003, the greater Washington D.C. area was terrorised by a Muslim sniper who killed 10 innocent people[23]. During the LA Riots and the post-Katrina civil unrest in New Orleans, gangs used stolen rifles to snipe at police and civilians alike. Most recently, in 2016, a domestic terrorist with military experience, killed five police officers in Dallas with a sniping attack.[24]

---

[23] https://www.history.com/this-day-in-history/washington-d-c-sniper-john-muhammad-convicted

We cannot pretend that the thugs and criminal gangs will *play fair* and not use sniping as a means to terrorise a community and take out sentries and security personnel. Sniper attacks are often used as a prelude to an assault or to force security to pull back therefore becoming less vigilant and effective.

To combat hostile sniper activity, the CIDC will need dedicated counter-snipers (CS) and personnel in overwatch positions. Once more, if you have experienced military veterans or law enforcement who have been trained in this capacity, you are fortunate. Minus the previous persons, leadership will need to recruit men who are both skilled in marksmanship and are highly trained/experienced observers.

---

[24] https://www.reuters.com/article/us-texas-crime/no-charges-for-dallas-officers-who-killed-sniper-with-robot-bomb-idUSKBN1FK35W

Counter-snipers and security overwatch personnel must be selected from the most experienced, skilled and mature members of the CIDC security element. The men on the ground must have absolute faith that the very best men are watching their backs.

Those in a CS position, again, must be able to make split second decisions that come down to literally life or death choices. Hesitation or second-guessing may cost the lives of friendly personnel, while a bad decision can also lead to catastrophe.

There is no room for bravado or braggadocio when it comes to the CS element. We are looking for cool customers who have the experience and maturity to make the absolutely correct decision based upon real world information that is playing out in minutes and seconds. There is a reason why trained military snipers are considered an elite class. They earn that reputation everyday.

Chapter 9 Conclusion

I fully understand that some who read this book may be skeptical as to whether or not community members could actually be brought together to function as an effective team for the protection of the community. If you are living in a major metropolitan area where the city government controls every aspect of your life by taxation and/or regulation, it might be easy to fall into this mindset. The "9-1-1 Mentality" has been hammered into our collective minds for at least a full generation. People have been taught not to be self-sufficient, but to use the 9-1-1 System as the answer to all of their problems.

The helpless victim mentality has been perpetuated by politician police chiefs who tell the citizens to simply give in to criminals, be good witnesses (victims) and call them afterward. Both the Chiefs of Oakland[25] and

Los Angeles[26] California have recently given such dangerous advice to the people living under their rule.

The Volunteer Spirit

In what I believe was a fortuitous situation, as I was preparing this final chapter, I witnessed genuine community volunteerism and cohesiveness in action. One morning, my dog was at the front window of the house, freaking out in a way that let me know someone was outside. When I went to the window, I saw two vehicles from the volunteer fire department and two privately owned trucks. They were blocking off my street. When I stepped outside to inquire as to what was going on, one of the volunteer firemen yelled, "The air ambulance is coming." Sure enough, sixty seconds later, a red and

25 https://abc7news.com/oakland-police-chief-leronne-armstrong-chinatown-opd/10346747/

26 https://www.thetruthaboutguns.com/lapd-tells-citizens-we-cant-help-you-so-cooperate-and-comply-with-criminals-and-be-a-good-witness/

white helicopter had landed on the street in front of my house. Another minute or two later, the local squad (ambulance) pulled up beside the helicopter.

The area in which I choose to live is a small, rural community and such a sight is rare indeed. From my porch, I watched as at least a dozen of my neighbors assisted in various ways. When it was all over, it occurred to me that of the dozen plus people milling about, the only ones who were being paid were the single sheriff's deputy and the two air ambulance personnel. The squad personnel and the firemen were all local volunteers who were helping, not because someone was paying them but, from a sense of community responsibility. I might add that this occurred in the winter and it was freezing cold outside while these neighbors were assisting their community.

While a Citizens Irregular Defense Corps is a different type of animal from a local volunteer fire department or EMS service, it is the spirit of the men and women in those organizations into which we hope to tap. Despite what you have come to believe, there is still a genuine spirit of community in the United States of America, at least in rural America. As a CIDC leader, it is your responsibility to foster and support that spirit of community from those whom you will be assisting and leading.

Continued Education

No book or manual can provide one hundred percent of the education and information you will need to keep your community safe and secure during an emergency or crisis. What I have attempted to do here is produce a text with enough information to help you make good decisions and to inspire you to continue to learn and grow.

In my three decades of experience, I have read innumerable military field and technical manuals. Most of these have been as exciting or interesting as watching paint dry. My hope throughout this guide has been to not only provide information, but historical perspective as well through the use of myriad footnotes. There are more references and footnotes in this book than any of my previous works and that was done deliberately. Please take the time to use the information to your benefit.

Although some might be disappointed at the lack of specific instructions, the truth is that the world is a very uncertain place, particularly at the point in time when these words are put to paper. I cannot predict the type of prolonged crisis or emergency with which your community will be faced. What I can tell you is that waiting until the crisis materializes to get prepared is a recipe for failure and disaster.

In addition to the suggested reading material at the end of this book, I would suggest that the reader study not only the strategies of General George Patton, but those of General Hal Moore as well. Read both "We Were Soldiers Once and Young"[27] and Moore's book on leadership, "Hal Moore on Leadership: Winning When Outgunned and Outmanned"[28].

---

[27] https://amzn.to/3Gz88QL

[28] https://amzn.to/33mTuOh

Also, I would suggest reading about the history of the following conflicts; the Norwegian Occupation during WWII, the Finnish Resistance Movement, the Citizens Irregular Defense Group during the Vietnam War, the Rhodesian Bush War, the French and Indian War and the American Revolutionary War. During all of these situations, citizens were called upon to defend their communities and nations.

Before I close this book and send you off to do good things, I wanted to insert the following lesson. This was written by my friend, Paul G. Markel. It is a good lesson for explaining why we do what we must do. I hope that you enjoy it as much as I have.

The Parable of the Rats

A farmer was setting rat traps in his barn and his young son was with him. "Papa, do you hate rats?" the boy asked his father. "No, I don't hate the rats. Why do you ask?" The little boy seemed confused. "If you don't hate them, then why do you kill them?" The farmer, realizing his son's confusion, sat the boy down on a bail of hay, took a deep breath and formulated his response.

"You see son, in our barn we have many animals that help us and feed us. The horses pull our wagons and our plows. The sheep give us wool that your mother spins and weaves and makes into clothing. Our cows give us milk to drink and the steers give us meat to eat so we can stay strong and healthy. But, you see, the rats do not do any of those things. When the rats come into our barns they chew on the ropes, the halters, and bridles for the horses

174

and ruin them. The rats get into the feed for the animals and eat it and they get into the wheat and grain that we use to make bread.They also carry diseases that can make the good animals sick."

"But one little rat doesn't eat that much corn." the little boy asserted. His father smiled knowingly. "You are right son, one rat all by itself won't eat that much corn, although they can still spread disease to our animals. The trouble with rats is that they never arrive alone and stay that way. If I let one rat live in our barn, soon there will be ten rats. If I ignore the rats, before long there will be a hundred rats and then more than you could count. Eventually, everything we have worked so hard for, our crops, our animals, even the barn itself will be eaten up, chewed up, and destroyed."

The look on the little boy's face showed he was understanding the lesson. His father summed it *up for him. "You see son, I cannot change the nature of the rats. They are going to try and eat our grain and destroy our property. A rat is going to be a rat. I don't hate the rats, but since they are not going to change, I have to kill them to protect all for which we have worked so hard."*

The farmer's son stood up and asked. "Will you show me how to set the traps?" "Yes son, of course. One day, killing the rats will be your responsibility."

About the Author

Nicolas Orr is the nom de plume for a civilized barbarian, a savage gentleman, with thirty plus years of operational and combat experience in the United States and overseas. The author has carried a gun during innumerable assignments worldwide as a member of the United States Military, as a Military Contractor, and Executive Protection Agent.

Other Books by Nicholas Orr:

- The Operator
- Sin City: The Operator Book 2
- Operation Diomedes: The Operator Book 3
- Operation White Feather Part 1: The Operator Book 4
- Operation White Feather Part 2: The Operator Book 5

Other Recommended Reading:

- The Patriot Fire Team Manual
- Patriot Fire Team Equipment Guide
- Patriot Fire Team Mission Planner

Made in the USA
Las Vegas, NV
08 July 2024